An Introduction to the Church's Liturgical Year

By Martin F. Connell

LOYOLAPRESS.

CHICAGO

LOYOLAPRESS.

3441 N. ASHLAND AVENUE
CHICAGO, ILLINOIS 60657
(800) 621-1008

Interior Design: Megan Keane DeSantis
Cover Design: Shawn Biner
Cover Art: Jason O'Malley

© 1997 Loyola Press

ISBN-13: 978-0-8294-1024-2
ISBN-10: 0-8294-1024-4

08 09 10 11 12 DataR 14 13 12 11 10 9 8 7 6 5

Contents

Introduction

After the meeting of the Roman Catholic bishops of the world during Vatican II, much about Catholic worship in the United States changed. For those old enough to remember, we think of the big changes: the move from Latin to the vernacular, English for most in this country; the introduction of lay ministries in the Sunday assembly—lectors, eucharistic ministers, greeters, etc.; the turning around of the altar so that the priest now faced the congregation. The assembly itself started participating rather than spectating. We sing, we process, we give and receive the sign of peace.

Other major elements of the Roman Catholic tradition, however, stayed much as they had, and one of these elements is our Catholic measurement of time within the year. This measurement is the liturgical year—the cycles and seasons, weeks and days by which we remember the presence of God in the past, celebrate it in the present, and anticipate the presence of God in the days to come and "at the hour of our death."

Because so little about the liturgical year changed, it might have fallen into the background of the things in our worship that have changed. Yet the wonders and complexities of the liturgical year can teach us a great deal about the presence of God in the history of Israel, in the life of Jesus of Nazareth and the early Church, and about the centuries of Church history from then until today.

The six chapters of this book explore the wonders and the complexities of our Roman Catholic understanding of time within the liturgical year. Chapter one begins with a reflection on how God has been present at various times in history and is present today. Here we will consider a few factors that have shaped our calendary.

Chapter two will examine the many "calendars" in the life of a Roman Catholic worshiper in the United States. It will consider the different measurements of time in the secular world and in the Church.

Chapter three will look to the highpoint of the liturgical year: the celebrations and seasons of Easter. Easter is not the beginning of the liturgical year (that happens at the beginning of Advent), but it is the supreme moment of God's presence and revelation to us. All of the Easter mysteries revolve around the presence of God in the community celebrating the initiation of new members.

Chapter four will consider the "first day of the week" for a Christian, Sunday, the day when the Christian community gathers and is renewed and reborn.

Chapter five will present the complex history of Christmas, Epiphany, and the seasons of Advent and Christmas. We will see here how many of the traditions of our American culture contradict the Catholic tradition about this time of the year.

Lastly, in chapter six, we examine the tradition of celebrating the lives of "those who have gone before us, marked with the sign of faith," the saints. Unlike the other issues, the tradition of liturgical celebrations in memory of the saints has changed a great deal since Vatican II, especially during the papacy of John Paul II. We will see how important it is for us to keep alive the memory of those who, though now dead, belong to our community of faith.

1 Time and the Presence of God

F ew things are so taken for granted as the passage of time. In a way time is so obvious as to be nearly invisible, yet for Christians, time has weighty meanings, meanings drawn from and made unique by the life of Jesus of Nazareth. We know by faith that Jesus was the Son of God, but in his earthly life Jesus was born into a specific culture during a particular time period, and a relatively short period of time when seen against world history in general. We can and indeed will find meaning in his incarnation into a particular culture with its own understanding of the presence of God in time.

One way in which these particularities are reflected in our faith is that Jesus' culture and his geographical region are embedded in the Scriptures that we hear proclaimed in the assembly at church every Sunday. We hear parables about wheat and tares, about sheep and wolves, and about other things that are foreign to most of our day-to-day experiences in North America. From the Hebrew Scriptures we ponder complex and enigmatic stories about the ancient Israelites. The culture of ancient Israel and of Jesus of Nazareth provide a foundation for the context of our Christian faith. Revelation about God comes at the specific times in which God is present, and understanding those times is necessary so that we can have access to the mysteries and the new life available to us by a life lived in the presence of God. Some times have great significance, even though the unfamiliar settings in which they emerged can make appreciating them difficult for us American Catholics.

THE LIFE OF JESUS AND THE LITURGICAL YEAR

Jesus lived 2,000 years ago. And, in the tradition of his parents, Joseph and Mary, Jesus was a Jew. While he criticized many of the Jewish religious leaders of his time, he also followed the Jewish faith and lived according to the conception of time of pious Jews in the first century. In the development of the Church after the death of Jesus, these Jewish observances of time, of significant moments in each year, were to have deep influences on the Christian tradition. These influences still continue today.

As we hear about the places in the life of Jesus—Jerusalem, Capernaum, Nazareth, Bethlehem, Golgotha, and so on—we also hear of significant times in his life—the Sabbath, Passover, the Feast of Unleavened Bread, and others. These formed the nucleus from which the Christian calendar grew.

THE LITURGICAL YEAR AND CHRISTIAN INITIATION

The Christian year has been shaped according to the life of the historical Jesus of Nazareth and the calendar of his own faith. But another factor was equally important in the emergence and development of the liturgical year: the initiation of Christians. Within the past few decades, following the reforms of Vatican II, the Church has implemented the Rite of Christian Initiation of Adults, the "RCIA," as it is commonly called.

This process of initiating Christians seems quite new to us, but it is actually a restoration of an initiation practice of the very early Church. For the first four or five hundred years of Christianity, a long and rigorous process of adult initiation was common. Communities of faith labored to support those who were preparing for initiation (they were and are now once again called "catechumens") and to welcome those who were most recently initiated (the "neophytes"). In the lives of the catechumens and the neophytes, communities witnessed concretely how the life, death, and resurrection of Jesus made a significant difference—a conversion, if you will—in the lives of Christians, in communities of faith, and even in the life of the world.

The paschal mystery as it was mediated for us in the life of the human being Jesus of Nazareth is no different from the paschal mystery of the initiated in the Church of the ancient world. There was no wide margin between the believers' understanding of the life of Jesus and their experience of the process of initiation in the Church. The paschal mystery that culminated in the life, death, and resurrection of the Savior was the very same impetus and reason for the initiation of catechumens into communities of faith.

The life of the risen Savior was most evident in the new Christians who had emerged from the waters of baptism, who had been anointed with the sacred chrism of confirmation, and who had shared in the eucharistic banquet. It was unthinkable in the early Church to separate the human life of the Savior and the experience of the risen Lord in those being initiated.

PAST, PRESENT, AND FUTURE

By commemorating the historical life of Jesus, we embrace the *past* as a component of our Christian faith. By working with the catechumens and celebrating their initiation each year at the Easter Vigil, we embrace the *present* as an essential component of our Christian faith. Joining our assembly at Sunday Eucharist is also a major aspect of the present that we embrace in our Catholic faith. Finally, by putting the Christian past and the life of Jesus together with the Christian present in the initiation process and in Sunday Eucharist, we anticipate the third component by which we measure Christian time: the future.

The life of Jesus and the life of faith—which we discover in our parish's celebration of initiation and the other sacraments—point us toward the life in God that we will meet in its fullness when we ourselves die. We have an assurance about the *future* from the glimpses of that life we discover in the life of Jesus of Nazareth and in the life of our own community of faith. Our faith also points us toward the end of time, when the Lord will return in glory. Be this tomorrow or millennia from now, the end will not bring fear or anxiety if we have celebrated the life of faith given to us in baptism.

Past, present, and future—all three are part of living out our Christian faith. And all three are reflected in the seasons and feasts of the Catholic liturgical year.

THE POPULARITY OF CHRISTIAN FAITH IN THE FOURTH CENTURY

What happened, you might be asking, between the early Church and the twentieth century that caused us to lose the experience and the understanding of the process of adult initiation?

While it is difficult to attribute the loss of the communal celebration of initiation to any one particular turn in the Church's history, one can say, in a sense, that it is a result of the time when the Church started to get "too big for its britches." This began to happen during the fourth century. When the Roman emperors themselves started not only to support Christianity but were themselves initiated into the faith, it became socially and even politically advantageous in the secular world to become a Christian.

Earlier, in the first few centuries of Christian life, being a Christian could often be a risk to one's life. Some Christians were tortured and even killed simply for being Christian. We have valuable accounts of early Christians being beaten and fed to wild beasts because of their faith. The blood of the martyrs, as one early Church leader expressed it, was the seed of the Church.

The spread of the faith led to the popularization of Christianity such that eventually the emperors themselves decided to become Christians. The emperor Constantine, who died in the year 336, was the first Roman emperor to become a Christian, and in the years following his empire, Christianity began to grow more rapidly. Perhaps it was when the powers-that-be themselves became Christian that others likewise flocked to the Church and made the lengthy and laborious initiation process untenable.

Once the ruler of the empire and a large percentage of the population were Christian, it became a social and political advantage to join the faith that had once been a reason for the end of a Christian's life. Once being a Christian had advantages attached to it, the faith itself became more attractive and grew in numbers.

ORIGINAL SIN

Another factor that surely affected the long process of initiation was a changed understanding of sin in human nature. Theologians in the fourth and fifth centuries began to articulate a nuanced notion of original sin as that sin that is part of human nature even before individuals themselves commit any personal sin. While we usually think of sin as a result of our own efforts or lapse, theologians in the fourth and fifth centuries began to teach that there is an aspect of sin that is inherent in human life completely apart from the personal sins one committed. This sin is that of Adam and Eve; this sin is "original sin," a type of sin that weighs down human life even in the innocence of infancy.

One effect of this changed understanding of sin and its relationship to human nature was that it inevitably changed the character and purpose of Christian initiation. People began to worry that, uninitiated, they might die in a state of original sin, independent of the worthy life that they might have lived. The doctrine of original sin maintained, and still does maintain, that no matter how virtuous and holy a life a Christian person lives, he or she is still influenced ("stained" is the more traditional description) by original sin, by the disobedience of our first parents.

A result of this theology was a growing fear that human beings might die before this original sin had been washed away in the baptismal waters of initiation. Little by little parents sought to have their children baptized before the children themselves had grown up and sought incorporation into a Christian church on their own. Eventually the fear that a child might die in a state of original sin led to the frequent and, eventually, widespread practice of baptizing children in infancy, often within a few weeks or even a few days of their birth. When the lives of infants were at stake after birth, the baptism took place immediately.

AN INITIATION-SHAPED CALENDAR

Although the Christian liturgical calendar reflects the time in the early Church when the process of initiation stretched throughout the year and was reflected deeply in the year, eventually the feasts related to the process of adult initiation remained even as the adult initiation itself disappeared. In fact, for most of Christian history, the feasts of the liturgical year stayed in place, even as the initiation of adults was no longer celebrated or, when celebrated, no longer a result of the initiation process in the parish community.

LOSS OF COMMUNITY IN THE PROCESS OF INITIATION

Many people can remember or have heard about the time before Vatican II when converts to Christianity were given instruction by the priest in the rectory and baptized in the church in a very brief ceremony with only a few family members present. The community of faith into which the persons were incorporated was completely absent.

There was no remembrance of the experience of the early Church, when initiation was not a discrete, disconnected rite, far away from the weekly celebration of the community of faith. Baptism was no longer seen as a supreme accomplishment and gift to the Church in general, or to this community of believers in particular. As a result of this separation, for over 1,000 years of Christian history baptism took place with virtually no more involvement of the community than the ministering of the priest for instruction and for a brief ceremony with a trickle of water as the efficacious sign of a radical change in values.

LOOKING AHEAD

Having briefly examined some of the intricacies that have shaped the Church's liturgical calendar, let's consider in the next chapter some of the ways an American Catholic might keep time. Then, in succeeding chapters, we'll explore in more detail the various seasons and cycles of the Church's liturgical year.

2 The American Catholic's Liturgical Year

Even though studying the liturgical year may seem like a rather simple matter—Easter, Christmas, saints' days, etc.—it is in fact difficult when the liturgical calendar is placed beside the other calendars of our lives. Believe it or not, measuring and observing times and seasons of the year—even though it is something we usually don't notice—can be quite a complicated matter for a Roman Catholic in the United States. There are various starts and finishes to the year, and a wide variety of days of significance in between those two. Some of the calendars are not only different but in conflict with one another. Let's look at the main measurements of time that we observe as American Catholics.

THIRTY DAYS HAS SEPTEMBER, APRIL, JUNE . . .

Perhaps the most fundamental calendar for the measurement of time in our lives is the basic division of time into minutes, hours, days, weeks, months, and years. This calendar is a constant in our lives. We might know *what* time it is or what day of the week it is or the date at a given moment, but we don't usually stop to question *why* it is that time, day, or date. But calendars have evolved throughout human history; in fact, the imposition or the modification of a way of measuring time was a display of a ruler's exalted status.

At numerous times in history, rulers, emperors, popes and, in more recent centuries, scientists have proposed new ways to measure and keep track of time that was better than the "old way." Back then such a change was made even more complex because communication was not as instantaneous or universal as it is today, so word of the changes in the measurement of time was slow. In small places where many cultures existed together, many calendars were observed in a rather narrow geographical space. As you can imagine, it was quite confusing when these cultures interacted. For better or worse, the simultaneously different ways of measuring time in the world are probably fewer today than ever throughout history, a result, most likely, of the globalization and standardization that have come about from economic and communication advances.

The way of measuring time in hours, days, weeks, months, and years is not, however, unique to us as Americans. Even though the time of day does vary according to the different times of the rising and setting of the sun on different continents and time zones, the increments in which time is divided up are fairly universal. Most of the countries with which we trade and communicate use similar ways and quantities for measuring time.

THE "AMERICAN" CALENDAR

In addition to the universal calendar, we in the United States also mark days of importance for ourselves as American citizens. As Americans, we have days of unique significance in our lives, days that do not bear the same meaning in the lives of Europeans (with whom many of us share a great deal of culture) or in the lives of Canadians and Mexicans (with whom we share a continent).

Examples of such uniquely American days are Thanksgiving, the Fourth of July, Presidents' Day, Memorial Day,

Labor Day, and so on. As we discovered not many years ago when Martin Luther King Day was brought to the cultural fore, the introduction of these days into the American calendar is not always appreciated equally. Because time is such a fundamental element of human life, all changes in the calendar are met with resistance.

The American calendar is observed by those who live here or who are in communication with those who live here. This group, though still in the hundreds of millions, is a smaller subset of the globe's people than those who divide up the months, weeks, days, and hours in the same increments that we do. A still narrower subset of time-keepers is made up of persons who are conscious of the significant days in their own personal history. For these people theirs is a unique way of keeping time for every human being.

OUR PERSONAL CALENDAR

Before moving into the distinctly Christian ways of keep-ing time, we can be mindful of the events in our own per-sonal lives. This last measurement embraces the days of the year that are important to us as individuals. Such days would include our birthday; the birthdays of our family members, loved ones, and friends; and perhaps the anniversary of our parents as well as, for many children, the days when our parents separated or divorced.

We would also keep track of the days when important persons in our lives died—our great grandparents, our grandparents, our aunts and uncles, mothers and fathers, brothers and sisters, and our friends. Each individual per-son has a unique "calendar" with which to remember sig-nificant times, persons, and experiences of his or her life.

Perhaps you had never before thought so consciously about the different ways time is measured around you and indeed the way you keep time for yourself. It's a two-way street: The way you keep time shapes your life, and the way you live your life influences the way in which you measure time.

Even before we've moved into considering the Christian cycles of measuring time, we've already found three cycles—universal, national/cultural, and personal—with which our years and days are measured and celebrated. At times these may be complementary to one another, and they may also be in conflict. To these we now add the distinctive measurements of time in the Church.

CHRISTIAN TIME

THE TEMPORAL CYCLE: THE SEASONS OF THE LITURGICAL YEAR

In addition to the secular ways of keeping time, we have three more ways that are uniquely important for us as Christians and, more specifically, as Roman Catholics. The first measurement of time for us as Catholics is the division of the year according to liturgical seasons and celebrations. The *temporal* cycle, as it's called, comes from the Latin word meaning times or seasons. Many Christian churches and denominations also observe these seasons, and as a result the liturgical year is common to many Christians we know, even those who do not worship in a Catholic community.

From the beginning to the end of the liturgical year, there are really only a few such seasons. In chronological order these seasons are Advent, Christmastime, the first season of Ordinary Time, Lent, the Triduum (literally, "the three days" of Easter—meaning Holy Thursday, Good Friday, and Holy Saturday), the Easter season (from Easter to Pentecost), and the relatively long second season of Ordinary Time, which fills in the nearly half-year gap from Pentecost to the beginning of Advent of the following liturgical year.

One of the most noticeable things about taking a bird's eye view of the liturgical year is how very out of balance it is. For one thing, the seasons themselves are of such odd and dissimilar lengths: Advent is approximately four weeks, Christmastime is about two or three weeks, Lent is 40 days, the Triduum is three days, Eastertime lasts 50 days, and Ordinary Time makes up over one half of the year. With the two main festal cycles of Easter and Christmas concentrated in the first half of the liturgical year, we find the second half of the year to be repetitious or—if you are a liturgical minister, a choir member, a musician, or a liturgical planner—a relief! How can this be?

Well, the same can be said about the imbalanced concentration of seasons in the first half of the liturgical year as can be said of human life in general: It's messy. That's a large part of the wonder and the puzzlement of studying it!

For now the important thing to recognize about these seasons is that they are not, for the most part, determined by the *date* on which the days occur. Rather they were and are determined by cosmological events such as the measurement of light and darkness, the sun and the moon, or by religious events of ages past. We will consider these cosmological happenings and religious antecedents more closely when we consider the individual Church seasons more closely over the next chapters.

THE CALENDAR OF THE SAINTS

The next Christian reckoning of time is not measured by the liturgical seasons or by the sun and the moon but by the calendar of the saints. The days in this "Sanctoral" Cycle (coming from the Latin words *sanctus* and *sancta*, meaning "saint") are attached to dates rather than to days of the week or to seasons.

We know, for example, that the Feast of Saint Martin of Tours—whom we usually find portrayed in soldier's garb, perched high on a horse, cutting his cape for a poor man —will always fall on November 11.

TIME ACCORDING TO THE LECTIONARY

After Vatican II the Church issued a new Lectionary, the ordered book of readings from which the liturgy's Scriptures are proclaimed. The Lectionary's rendering adds still another conception of time to those we've already seen. The most distinctive configuration of the Lectionary's rendering of time is that it is not an annual cycle but a three-year plan. This plan was laid out in order for the faithful to hear a fuller selection proclaimed from the many books of the Bible. The three-year basis comes from the first three Gospels of the New Testament, and each of these texts— Matthew, Mark, and Luke—correspond with one year: Matthew for Year A, Mark for Year B, and Luke for Year C.

The Bible and the Lectionary

The shape of the Lectionary comes from an ancient Church practice of *lectio continua*, a Latin term that describes the successive reading through books of the Bible from Sunday to Sunday. If you study the content of the readings as they are matched up on given Sundays and feasts in the Lectionary, you will find that the first reading often will echo some image, character, or idea of the Gospel, as is the Church's intention. The second reading often stands on its own, chosen as a reading from a letter of Paul or another letter of the New Testament.

The Lectionary as an Essential Manifestation of "Catholicism"

The basic plan of the Lectionary for Catholics is universal. The readings proclaimed in your church on a particular Sunday are the same as those proclaimed in Catholic churches all over the globe. The Lectionary is one of the main things that makes our liturgy so "catholic," or universal.

Not only are the readings the same as those in other Catholic churches, but the revision of the Roman Catholic Lectionary was so well received that other Churches began to follow in the three-year Lectionary cycle. So not only are the readings the same in Catholic churches, but as time has passed other Christian churches have adopted the Catholic Lectionary.

Now that we have just reviewed the many overlapping cycles, seasons, and celebrations that bear on a practicing Catholic's conception of time, we can start looking at particular aspects of the liturgical year.

3 Easter

Even though Easter is not the *beginning* of the Roman Catholic liturgical year, it is the highpoint of the year. Easter is the celebration of the paschal mystery, coming from the word *pascha*, which means "Easter."

There are a number of aspects of the paschal mystery incorporated into the celebration of Easter that makes it so embracive. One of these aspects, and perhaps the one that comes to the minds of most Christians when they think about Easter, is the memory of the life, death, and resurrection of Jesus.

Another aspect of the Easter mysteries is the presence of the risen Christ beyond the time of his human journey. In the memorial acclamation of the eucharistic prayer at Mass we sing: "Christ has died, Christ is risen, Christ will come again." Alleluia. That we proclaim that "Christ *is* risen" emphasizes that the Resurrection—indeed the whole of the paschal mystery—is not a past event that we merely commemorate. It is part of our lives today, part of the life of the Church since the days of the community that was formed around Jesus of Nazareth, continuing and being built up in love as you stand in your assembly each Sunday at your own parish.

THE INITIATION OF CHRISTIANS

Your parish community celebrates still another aspect of the celebration of Easter: the community gathered around the font to initiate and welcome into its fold the catechumens, those who have prepared for this entrance into the community of faith. With adults this initiation should happen on the night of the Easter Vigil. Gone are the days when preparation for becoming a Christian could happen by the person to be initiated meeting with one of the parish priests in the rectory office for instruction. Instruction—or "catechesis," as it's often called these days—is merely one part of the process of initiation.

From the witness that the parish has given to the person thinking about becoming a Christian, that person has discerned that in this community he or she will commit to the faith, and the parish celebrates that commitment at the Easter Vigil.

With the neophytes who commit themselves to the community, we who are already initiated renew our commitment to the Body of Christ. This renewal of our baptismal promises in the celebration of the initiation of the catechumens-become-neophytes is still another aspect of the paschal mystery that we observe and celebrate at Easter.

THE SECOND COMING

There is another aspect to what we do at the Easter celebration: We anticipate the final coming of the Lord in glory. This may be at our death or at the end of the world, and we look for this end at Easter.

WHY THE BIG FUSS OVER THE INITIATION OF ADULTS AT EASTER?

Since Vatican II the newest part of the Easter celebration is the initiation of adults into the parish community. Many Christians who were baptized as infants are puzzled by the fuss that is made over those who are initiated as adults at the Easter Vigil. So what's the big deal? they might rightly wonder. Again, there are several aspects to this, and the

Rite of Christian Initiation of Adults (RCIA) itself provides much of our guide.

For one thing, we see that the RCIA does not take
place as an isolated and instantaneous moment or as a
magical spell removed from the support of the community
to which the initiated are joined. Rather, the rite takes
months, sometimes years, to accomplish. And it all gets
started at God's initiative. God does the inviting, the cate-
chumen responds, and the local community is the instru-
ment and the witness. Let's briefly look at the stages of the
adult initiation process and its implication for the parish
and for those of us who were in fact baptized before we
were ever conscious of having been made a Christian.

INQUIRY AND EVANGELIZATION

The first stage of the RCIA process is the period of
Inquiry and Evangelization. There is no commitment
here; the candidate approaches the community, inquiring
about the faith and the practices of that particular community. The church leaders respond to the inquiry with evangelization, with the Good News, and with answers to the
questions that the inquirer brings. If all moves peacefully
and compatibly, this period, whose length is not fixed,
ends with a rite of acceptance, after which the inquirer is
enrolled into the Order of Catechumens.

THE ORDER OF CATECHUMENS AND THE RITE
OF ELECTION

This second stage is similarly of an indeterminate length.
This period involves catechesis and rites that accompany
the catechesis. All stages of the RCIA have a mix of both
instruction and rites to familiarize the candidate with the
practices of the Church. This second period ends with the
Rite of Election, after which the candidate is set on the

path toward initiation at the Easter Vigil. The Rite of Election takes place in the community and usually about six weeks before the Vigil, during which the initiation rite will happen. Some bishops bring the elect to the cathedral of the diocese or archdiocese for the Rite of Election.

The initiation ball begins to roll more speedily now because the third stage coincides with the period of Lent during the Church year. It is a time of purification and enlightenment and happens during the 40 days of Lent.

THE EASTER VIGIL AND THE EASTER SEASON

The fourth part is not really a stage but a rite: It is the Rite of Initiation itself at the Easter Vigil, about which more will be said below.

The fifth part of the process extends throughout the 50-day period of the Easter season; it is the period of mystagogy. This is the time for the post-initiation catechesis, for those who have been initiated to reflect back on the experience with others in the community. It is a time for deepening the Christian experience by sharing it with others, a time, as the *Introduction to the RCIA* says, "for spiritual growth, and for entering more fully into the life and unity of the community" (7). The period of mystagogy ends near Pentecost, at the end of the Easter season.

WHAT THE RCIA MEANS FOR THE ALREADY BAPTIZED

In the *General Introduction to Christian Initiation*, we read that "[i]n the sacraments of Christian initiation we are freed from the power of darkness and joined to Christ's death, burial, and resurrection. We receive the Spirit of filial adoption and are part of the entire people of God in the celebration of the memorial of the Lord's death and resurrection" (1). This is quite a solemn and weighty moment that we celebrate, yet for those of us baptized as infants, the weight of our incorporation in the death, burial, and resurrection of Christ and into the entire people of God takes a long time to sink in, if it ever really does.

At the Easter Vigil the soon-to-be initiated are asked about what they seek in coming to the Church. Though the question is addressed directly to the catechumens, we, too, are prompted to reconsider our own reason for being there and the depth (or shallowness) of our incorporation into the entire people of God in our parish and in the universal Christian Church.

THE 40 DAYS OF LENT

The season of Lent is the period of the most intense preparation of those to be initiated, who by that point have celebrated the Rite of Election. They indeed are the "elect," those chosen for and on their way to the life-changing waters of baptism. Those who remember the days when Lent was simply the 40 days of stark living, our time of fasting and abstinence as we approached Easter, might wonder why that has been changed.

Why, one might wonder, has the Church eliminated the part of Lent with which we were most familiar (abstaining from meat on Fridays and general avoidance of indulgent activity) and added a part with which we Catholics are so unfamiliar (this attention to the catechumens and the elect)? The truth of the matter is that the aspect with which we were unfamiliar is the most ancient part of the 40 days of Lent. Lent evolved to be what we remember it as *because* it had earlier been the period during which the elect were anticipating the initiation rites. We have not recently added the RCIA to the 40 days; the

RCIA of the ancient Church was the very reason why the 40 days became part of the Church's liturgical year!

In the reconfiguration of the Church's calendar after Vatican II, the Church restored not only the very ancient adult initiation process but also the readings that the early Church proclaimed during the Sundays of preparation throughout the 40 days, particularly on the Third, Fourth, and Fifth Sundays of Lent. There are three Gospel stories that were proclaimed to the elect and to their parishes in the ancient Church: the stories of the woman at the well (John 4:5–42), the man born blind (John 9:1–41), and the raising of Lazarus (John 11:1–44). Any parish that celebrates the RCIA proclaims these readings on the Third, Fourth, and Fifth Sundays of Lent.

Each of these stories tells of the progressive journey of a person into the mystery who is Christ himself. So, too, would our lenten disciplines of self-denial and abstinence, if they are done in the right spirit. They are not ends in themselves, but they are means to another end: union with Christ and with the Church in conjunction with those about to be baptized. Our journey with them is for us a renewal of faith and of life.

The fasting and abstinence of pre-Vatican II days became so as the process of the catechumenate progressed through history. The missing piece, however, and quite an oddity it is, is that the later aspects of the 40 days remained even though the initiation process itself had long ago disappeared! The baptism of infants became the normative way that people became Catholic. The ascetic and penitential character of the season, however, in place from the days of adult initiation, stayed in place for hundreds and hundreds of years after the initiation process for adults had been virtually erased.

THE SACRED TRIDUUM

The Easter Triduum (a Latin word that comes from the joining of two other Latin words meaning "three," *tres*, and "day," *dies*) refers to what is now the core span of the liturgical year.

The "Three Days" refers to the specific span of time that each year begins on Holy Thursday evening at the celebration of the Mass of the Lord's Supper and ends three days later at the celebration of evening prayer on Easter Sunday. In between that beginning and end of the Three Days each parish celebrates the Good Friday liturgy of the Lord's Passion and the Easter Vigil.

The Three Days of Easter as the heart of the liturgical year were not in place from the start of Christianity. For the first three or four centuries of Christian history—from the death of Jesus until the time when Christianity became the religion of the empire—the main Easter celebration was the Easter Vigil alone, and this liturgy centered not on the resurrection of Christ (as it does today) but on the passion and death. It is very possible that the word *pascha*, which today is the word for Easter in Romance languages, such as French (*Pâques*), Spanish (*Pascua*) and Italian (*Pasqua*), is derived from the Greek word *paschein*, which means "to suffer." Only in the fourth century do we find evidence of the other liturgies of the Triduum, i.e., Holy Thursday and Good Friday.

Although many Christians think that Lent spans the entire season from Ash Wednesday until the Vigil liturgy of Easter, the 40 days actually end earlier in the day of Holy Thursday. The 40 days of Lent bring us not to the Vigil but to the edge of the most sacred three days of the year, the Triduum.

One might wonder why the Easter celebration went from being one celebration to being a three-day span of celebrations. Once Christianity was the religion of the empire, Christians no longer had to exist in hiding. Persecutions of Christians, which was public entertainment in some parts of the ancient world, ceased, and Christians could worship in public. The public character of Christianity extended to the family of the emperor, and the mother of Constantine (the first Christian emperor) became a Christian. Tradition tells us that she, St. Helena, became a Christian before her imperial son, and part of the influence on the emperor's conversion to the faith came from his own mother's devotion.

Tradition also tells us that St. Helena led a tour of the Holy Land, that small part of the world in which Jesus lived his human life. While there, Helena and her relic-seeking entourage found what tradition claims was the true cross of the Crucifixion. Attention to the places of Jesus' life and death led to attention to the times of the life and death of Jesus. Believers started reading the New Testament and sought to have the liturgical calendar reflect what is found there. Attention to the chronology embedded in the Gospels, therefore, led to having the Triduum displace the earlier single main celebration.

The death of Jesus was no longer the central narrative of the Easter Vigil, but the narrative of Jesus' death was moved to the Friday just before, the day that the first three Gospels tell us Jesus died. The same Gospels describe the Last Supper of the night before, and so Holy Thursday emerges as both the evening of the Last Supper (again using the first three Gospels as the source for this) and the footwashing rite (not described in Matthew, Mark, or Luke but only in the Gospel of John).

THE 50 DAYS

As Christians we usually think of Pentecost as the fiftieth day after Easter, counting both Easter Sunday and Pentecost Sunday. Yet Pentecost is derived from a word meaning "fifty" (think of pentagon, a figure with five sides), and it earlier referred not to the fiftieth day and the end of the Easter season but to the entire 50-day span of the celebration of Easter during it.

Within the past few years it seems as if the Church has given a new designation for these days; they are now the days of mystagogy for the newly initiated. Yet the process of initiation is not a new, added aspect of the Easter season, but it is the very reason why the season came into being in the early Church. But when the process of the initiation of adults ended, the Church lost the reason for the season, even as its meaning—joy, renewal, celebration —survived. We lost the experience, but the meaning of the experience continued for centuries.

The Church teaches that these spans of time are not a series of discrete celebrations; rather they are a single, extended celebration. The *General Norms for the Liturgical Year* says: "The fifty days from Easter Sunday to Pentecost are celebrated as one feast day, sometimes called 'the great Sunday'" (22).

If we accept that Easter and its seasons are as they are because of their associations with the initiation process, we can see that well over one-quarter of the liturgies of the liturgical year revolve around supporting those who are being led to the waters of baptism or who are celebrating their entry into the Church during the 50 days. One-quarter of the year is a lot of devotion to initiation. This is a major shift from a few decades ago when initiation preparation was private, dissociated from the regular liturgical life of the parish, and almost entirely a matter of memorizing doctrine to the pastor's or priest's satisfaction.

4 Sunday

Sunday is the day of our most frequent contact with the Body of Christ in the assembly of our church. Sunday, the "first day of the week," as the Gospel writers describe it, is the day on which we are renewed, when we come face-to-face with the presence of God in the assembled people with whom we celebrate week after week. Sunday is the day when Christians most often experience their reception of the bread and the wine that in the liturgy become the real Body and Blood of Christ.

Even though this has been so for almost all of Christian history, the New Testament is surprisingly quiet about what Christians of the early Church did when they came together on Sunday, if indeed they did so. Part of the ambiguity about Sunday worship according to the New Testament is that for the first few decades after the death of Jesus, his followers were all practicing Jews. Many continued their ritual observances of Judaism in earnest, while gathering with other Jews who also had come to believe that Jesus was the Messiah, the Son of God.

THE ADMISSION OF THE GENTILES

What the New Testament does shed light on and inform us about the changes in Christian practices is the controversy about admitting Gentile (non-Jewish) believers into the Christian assemblies. Perhaps you can remember hearing some of the letters of Paul in the second readings in which he speaks about the Jews, who—like Paul himself—

were considered the "righteous heirs of faith" because of their observance of the Law. But in the end Paul—unlike other apostles, such as Peter and James and other authors of the New Testament—concluded that it was not observance of the Law of the Torah that made one a Christian but the gift of faith. And the Gentiles, though not circumcised and not followers of the Law of Moses, could be coheirs of the faith given by God and would remain so.

FROM SABBATH TO SUNDAY

Until the admission of the Gentiles in the first century, all Christians had continued their observance of the Law, including the rites in the Temple on Saturdays, the seventh day, the Sabbath. Once the Gentiles were admitted, however, the ritual practices of the followers of Jesus were free to move away from Jewish practices.

Once the observance of the Jewish Sabbath (Saturday) was no longer a requirement for Christians, it is likely that Sunday began to emerge as the day for celebrating the Eucharist. This change probably happened gradually in the second half of the first century. Moreover, Sunday not only was the day on which Christians *could* celebrate their rites but, once the numbers of Christians increased, Sunday was the day that marked their celebrations as distinct from the Sabbath observance of the Jews.

SUNDAY IN THE GOSPELS

The Gospels were written in the second half of the first century, during this period when the Gentiles were coming to the Christian faith. It is not likely that any of the writers of the books of the New Testament were first-person eyewitnesses to the life of Jesus. The apostle Paul, whose letters are the most ancient texts of the New Testament, knew and met with the apostles—such as Peter—

who had been first-person, face-to-face followers of the Lord. But as he himself admits, he was not an eyewitness to the events. The Gospel writer Luke also admits to receiving the narratives from those who were eyewitnesses (see Luke 1:1–4), admitting in the same place that he, too, was not among these people.

THE DAY OF THE RESURRECTION

In the Gospels we do not find Sunday as a day for assembling the followers of Jesus, but we discover in all four Gospels that the Resurrection took place on Sunday. (See Matthew 28:1–7, Mark 16:1–8, Luke 24:1–8, and John 20:1–18.) In addition to being the day on which Jesus had been raised from the dead, the first day of the week was also the day on which Jesus appeared to the disciples after the Resurrection.

As we have seen so far, on Easter, both in the early Church and today, there is a fuzzy border between speaking of the resurrected Christ who "was raised and sits at the right hand of the Father" and the resurrected Christ who is present in the Eucharist, in the community assembled around the altar in the Sunday Eucharist. The fuzziness is advantageous because we know from the promises of Christ that he is fully present in both. They are two sides of the coin that is our faith. We cannot so overemphasize and overcelebrate one at the expense of the other.

We cannot, on the one hand, think of the Resurrection as merely an event in the life of the historical Jesus. That is wholly true, yet the Resurrection continues in the life of the Church. We experience the Resurrection when we celebrate the initiation of new members into our communities at the Easter Vigil. We experience the Resurrection when we celebrate the baptism of infants. We experience the Resurrection whenever we celebrate the sacraments. And we experience the Resurrection whenever we bond with those we love because they are gifts of God. Yet these experiences are only one side of the coin.

The Resurrection also was part of the experience of Jesus, the Son of God who shared his human life with us by his incarnation. And so the Resurrection also was part of the experience of the paschal mystery in the life of Jesus two millennia ago. That is the other side of the coin that is the Christian faith.

PENTECOST

The New Testament not only gives witness to Sunday as the day of the Resurrection, but it is clear from witnesses that Sunday also is the day of the coming of the Holy Spirit. The Easter season in our liturgical year, as we saw in a previous chapter, is the 50-day period from Easter Sunday until, and including, Pentecost Sunday, the day on which the Church celebrates the coming of the Holy Spirit and the reception of the gifts that come to us from the Spirit. This is the last Sunday of the Easter season, the day on which our Easter joy is complete.

LUKE ON PENTECOST

Luke, the author of a Gospel and the Acts of the Apostles, gives us the most detailed account of the original Christian Pentecost Sunday. His account provides a strong testimony to the strength we receive in the gifts of the Spirit, and this strength is the power that we receive also at the Sunday Eucharist we celebrate each week. The first section of his account is what artists through the centuries have taken for their representations of this event:

> *Suddenly there came from the sky a noise like a strong driving wind, and it filled the entire house in which they were. Then there appeared to them tongues as of fire, which parted and came to rest on each one of them. And*

they were all filled with the holy Spirit and began to speak in different tongues, as the Spirit enabled them to proclaim.

—Acts 2:2–4

The gifts of the Spirit, the power of God, come to us not only on Pentecost Sunday but in the mystery of faith that we celebrate at the altar.

PETER ON PENTECOST

Immediately after this event, Peter stands up in the midst of the amazed crowd looking on and proclaims:

"It will come to pass in the last days," God says,
 "that I will pour out a portion of my spirit
  upon all flesh.
 Your sons and your daughters shall prophesy,
  your young men shall see visions,
  your old men shall dream dreams.
Indeed, upon my servants and my handmaids
 I will pour out a portion of my spirit in those days,
  and they shall prophesy.
And I will work wonders in the heavens above
 and signs on the earth below:
  blood, fire, and a cloud of smoke.
The sun shall be turned to darkness,
 and the moon to blood,
 before the coming of the great and splendid day of
  the Lord,
and it shall be that everyone shall be saved who calls on
 the name of the Lord."

—Acts 2:17–21

After Peter's speech, we see that "those who accepted his message were baptized, and about three thousand persons were added that day" (2:41).

The boldness of Peter should cause us to anticipate the gifts of the Spirit in our own lives, enabling us to speak confidently to strangers about the power of God present to us in the Church. We, too, might follow the example of the "young men and women" of the reading above, of the prophets and dreamers, young and old.

THE LITURGY OF THE WORD

Because Jesus of Nazareth—who ate and drank with the disreputable, who befriended and loved those who were the most dejected, who healed the sick and raised the dead—is not present to us as he was to those who shared his company as a human being, we harken to the stories of the Bible that have preserved his life in our tradition.

Since Vatican II the Church has returned to the proclamation of the Word of God as a major element of our Sunday Eucharist. These stories are part of the celebration in which we participate in the Sunday gathering. In faith we trust and know that Christ is present in the proclamation of the Word and the preaching as he is present in the community gathered at the table to break and eat the bread and to pour and drink the wine. Because Catholics have today become as accustomed to reading and studying the Word of God as many of their Christian neighbors raised in more biblical denominations, we can open up the Scriptures as a guide for our lives and spiritualities.

One way in which we can do this is by preparing for hearing the Sunday readings. We can either purchase a Lectionary or jot down what readings will be used during the liturgy the following week. Perhaps you might join a Scripture study group, which would enable you to share your interest in Scripture with like-minded believers.

SUNDAY AS THE DAY FOR RENEWING OUR BAPTISMAL COMMITMENT

If you have ever been to the Easter Vigil when the elect are being initiated, you would have noticed that three of the seven sacraments take place. After declaring their intention to the assembled community, the elect are baptized. Then they are anointed with oil, receiving the sacrament that we call confirmation.

The end of their initiation brings them to the table of the Lord for receiving the Body and Blood of Christ in the bread and the wine. This is the sacrament in which we physically participate with them. That order of reception —baptism, confirmation, Communion—while foreign to the order by which most Catholics are initiated—is the way the early Church initiated its members.

They were first washed in the waters of baptism; then they were sealed and strengthened by the anointing with oil; finally, they were brought to the table, where they celebrated the part of their initiation rite that would continue throughout the remainder of their Christian life, however long or short that may have been.

Most Catholics, however, received these same three sacraments, but with years in between each of them and in a different order—baptism, Communion, and then confirmation. Celebrating first Eucharist before we are "sealed" at confirmation can be an obstacle toward recognizing the meaning of the Eucharist in our day-to-day lives, for it is the repeatable aspect of our initiation, the final act of initiation that can always draw us back to the purifying and unifying waters by means of which we became Christians.

When the Eucharist is received as the final of the three sacraments of the initiation sequence, we understand it as the reminder of our initiation, the reminder of our leaving the world behind as we entered into the new world of

God's embrace. In the new world we are wedded to those whom we may never have met outside the life of faith. The celebration of the Sunday Eucharist is a regular reminder of the gift we received in the life of faith and of the difference it makes in appreciating and understanding both our present life and in life after death.

When initiation is celebrated as bath (baptism), anointing (confirmation), and finally food (Eucharist), we approach the table knowing that in doing so we cross the threshold from the life we lived before to the life we live and celebrate now with God, in our parishes, in our communities of quite ordinary people.

Going forth to the altar to receive the Body and Blood of Christ marks our lives as treasured by God, as divinized by the coming of Jesus Christ into this world, as incorporated into the life of the God who rescued us from the powers of darkness and brought us into the healing light of Christ. The celebration of the Sunday Eucharist is a bathing in the light of the world revealed to us in Jesus of Nazareth, the Son of God and Savior.

Celebrating the Eucharist in the Sunday assembly is an immediate connection to our baptism, whether or not we are consciously able to remember the event itself. We know that baptism brought us in Christ to life with God by the power of the Holy Spirit. We thank God with our whole heart for the rescue we receive from darkness and for the safety we now enjoy in our community of faith. Gathering for Eucharist with the other worshiping members of our parish is the sure link to life in God as we receive it by the ministry of our parish.

5 The Seasons of Christmas and Advent

There are two basic theories about the origins of Christmas. The first is usually called the *calculation hypothesis*, and the second is termed the *history-of-religions hypothesis*. We will look at them in that order.

THE CALCULATION HYPOTHESIS

In this hypothesis the origins of the Feasts of Christmas and Epiphany are intimately and intricately tied together. In the ancient world an event was seen as especially under God's providence and protection when that event took place on unique and coincidental dates of the calendar. In the early centuries of Christian history, for example, events in the life of Jesus about which the Scriptures provide no dating evidence—and these are many—often were attributed to the same date.

EASTER ON A CALENDAR DATE, NOT ALWAYS ON A SUNDAY

In the early years of the Christian faith the annual feast of Easter, the most supreme feast of Christian observance then and now, took place on the same date of the calendar. Today the feast *always* takes place on a Sunday (and its vigil, Saturday night), and the day itself is determined each year according to the changes in amounts of light and darkness at that time of year. So while the date changes in our own time, in early Christianity the date was constant.

The issue gets even a little bit more cloudy, however, when one comes to realize that as ancient civilizations came into contact with one another, their conceptions of time would have to be adjusted. There were different increments of time into which the day, the month, and the year were divided up and, moreover, there were different names for these spans of time. As Christianity came to spread rapidly through the ancient world in the first few centuries after the death of Jesus, the faith and its communities would have to become inculturated into the host civilization's conceptions of time.

Because of this, agreement about what the date of Easter actually was varied from place to place. This can seem rather unbelievable to us today because we ourselves have become more and more accustomed to the immediate communication of information all around the globe. But then even the date of Easter was observed at different times from place to place.

FROM EASTER TO CHRISTMAS

Easter was always a springtime feast, but some churches of the ancient world dated Easter at March 25; others dated the feast at April 6. You might be wondering, with good reason, why this is being raised in a chapter about Christmas. Well, because of the ancient notion about the calendrical simultaneity of events of divine and religious importance, ancient Christians thought that the death of Christ must have been calendrically coincident with his incarnation, the day on which Jesus took flesh. The date on which the angel appeared to Mary, which today we call the Feast of the Annunciation, was that date on which the Savior took flesh, the day on which Mary's pregnancy began.

The way this bears on our discussion of Christmas is that if March 25 (or April 6, for the others) was indeed the date of the Savior's *incarnation*—"taking flesh," as the word incarnation means—then the span of Mary's pregnancy, nine months, would place the birth of Jesus on December 25 (or, again, on January 6).

TWO DATES FOR THE SAVIOR'S BIRTHDAY?

How were the disagreements about the date of the birth of Jesus resolved? In the fourth century, as the number of Christians increased rapidly and the faith became the religion of the Roman Empire, churches began to celebrate their liturgies in public and the differences in their various conceptions of time became apparent.

Some churches—in general we can suggest that these churches were those on the eastern side of the Roman Empire (many of which today are the Orthodox churches)—celebrated the birth of Jesus on January 6. The others—those on the western side of the Roman Empire, in what is today Europe—celebrated the birth on December 25. In the fourth century the bishops of the communities whose dating traditions were in conflict resolved it by maintaining (or adopting) December 25 as the feast of the birth and by adopting January 6 as the Feast of the Epiphany.

THE HISTORY-OF-RELIGIONS HYPOTHESIS

The other possibility for the origins of Christmas is not as complex. As Christianity began to prosper in the early Church, it clashed with those who belonged to other religions. Many of the non-Christians of the Roman world were pagans.

THE UNCONQUERED SUN

In the year 274 the Roman emperor Aurelian established a pagan feast for the empire; it was the feast *natale solis*

inuicti, the feast of "the birth of the unconquered sun."
The emperor's purpose was to mandate a celebration for
worshiping the Syrian sun god Emesa. He ordered that
this feast be observed on December 25, during the time
of the winter solstice.

Solstice refers to the times of the year when the day is
longest or shortest. The word *solstice* comes from two
Latin words (*sol-stice*), which mean "sun" and "to stand
still." So the solstice refers to the time of year when the
sun seems to be indeed standing still, with the result that
the day is either long (the sun at its peak), which is the
winter solstice, or short (the sun at its lowest), which is the
summer solstice. Today, and since the advent of electricity,
the solstices do not affect the activities and livelihood of
our days as much as they did centuries ago.

Emperor Aurelian was probably both encouraging the
cult of Emesa, the Syrian sun god, and giving people some
public consolation at the time of the year's darkest and
coldest season. These days we have to bear in mind that
this is not the case everywhere around the world. In the
Southern Hemisphere of the globe, the solstices are
reversed: The longest day is at the time of the Northern
Hemisphere's shortest, and the reverse is true as well. This
has caused the churches in the Southern Hemisphere,
where Christianity has been long since established, to
reconsider and rewrite some of the imagery of the prayers
of these feasts, because they are effective only as they are
in sync with the seasonal changes that happen on the
Earth and in the fields.

THE UNCONQUERED SON

The Church in the early fourth century, perhaps seeking
to keep Christians from being attracted to the pagan feast
worshiping the Syrian sun god, marked December 25 as
the day of the birth of Jesus Christ. The Church was able

to do so with reference to a verse from the Hebrew Scriptures, which for the Roman world had been translated into Latin by that time. In the Book of the Prophet Malachi, chapter 4, verse 2 reads:

Et orietur vobis timentibus nomen meum sol iustitiae.

Church leaders found this verse, referring to the Messiah as the "sun of justice," *sol iustitiae*, a theological means for finding Jesus to be their unconquered sun. Thus was December 25 chosen as the feast of the birth of the Savior.

Each of the above theories about the origins of Christmas is both fascinating and complex. Perhaps it was a combination of the two that led to the end result, our marking the birth of the Savior on December 25. We'll have to leave it to the calendrical scholars to wrestle that out; we can be content with the information we have for now.

THE NEW TESTAMENT ON CHRISTMAS

It might seem to be something of a surprise that the New Testament does not give us more specific references than it does about the birth of the Savior. For one thing only the Gospels of Matthew and Luke mention the birth, and the Gospel of Luke is the one that for centuries has fed Christian imaginations about the night of Jesus' birth. (When Linus, for example, on the Charlie Brown Christmas special, recites the narrative of Jesus' birth from the Bible, the story that he tells is that which begins the story in the Gospel of Luke.)

Despite the many images and insights that these two Gospel writers provide, they are silent about the date or the time of the year. Church tradition, as always, steps in to fill in the data and catechize in the absence of dating details from Scripture.

THE BIRTH OF JESUS IN MATTHEW

According to the birth account in the Gospel of Matthew
—which focuses on Joseph more than on Mary—Joseph
had in fact already decided to divorce Mary (1:19). Knowing that the child she carried was not physically his own,
Joseph sought obedience to the Law. Then an angel
appeared to Joseph, and the angel encouraged him to take
Mary as his wife.

Time did not make the situation better. Soon after the
child's birth, after the Magi had come and worshiped the
newborn Savior, they told the parents that they had to
flee to escape the devious plans of the ruler. King Herod,
threatened by the power of the Son of God, sought to
kill the child. The story tells us that Mary, Joseph, and
the child were safe in their hiding place, but this did not
curb the ruler's fear, and he ordered that all children
under two years of age in and around Bethlehem were to
be slaughtered.

The fear, dislocation, and murder of this infancy narrative give the Christmas story quite a different character
than that usually associated with the mirth and good cheer
of this feast. It's not the kind of bedtime story that would
warm children's hearts and deepen their anticipation of
Christmas morning!

THE BIRTH OF JESUS IN LUKE

The narrative in Luke, which focuses on Mary rather than
Joseph, is not as threatening as the one in Matthew. Like
the whole of the Gospel of Luke, the infancy narrative
centers around the nearness of God to the poor and disen-
franchised. The intimate bond between the simultaneously
pregnant cousins, Elizabeth and Mary, is engaging and
compelling.

In Matthew it is Joseph to whom the angel appears
announcing the events that were about to take place. In

Luke it is Mary who receives the angel's greeting and announcement. A few sentences from the angel's announcement form the first half of the prayer that we know today as the Hail Mary:

> *Hail, Mary, full of grace; the Lord is with you.*
> *(see Luke 1:28)*
> *Blessed are you among women, and blessed is the fruit of*
> *your womb, Jesus. (see Luke 1:42)*

Instead of the regal Magi bearing gifts of gold, frankincense, and myrrh for the newborn Savior, the infancy narrative of Luke has the poor shepherds standing in their fields at night when they, too, hear an angel's message: "I proclaim to you good news of great joy that will be for all the people. For today in the city of David a savior has been born for you who is the Messiah and Lord" (2:10–11).

TRADITION COMBINES MATTHEW AND LUKE

In a sense these two infancy narratives provide wonderful images for our celebrations of the birth of Jesus. Our nativity sets under or near our Christmas trees usually mix the characters of the two tales, both Magi and shepherds.

Kept separate, the Magi and shepherds reflect the unique theologies and characterizations of Jesus in the two Gospels with birth narratives. Yet together all is not lost: We learn of the revelation of God in the incarnate Son, who comes to us in our many different situations in this world, be we like the smelly shepherds; the gift-bearing Magi; like Zechariah, the muted husband of Elizabeth; or the perplexed Joseph, wondering how he could possibly trust that it is the presence of God that could lead to such a complex situation.

These surprises in the stories of the birth of Jesus are at the heart of the feast. They lead us to think about the presence of God and the companionship of Jesus Christ in our own days, for our faith teaches that God is no less present to us than in the days when Jesus walked in ancient Israel with his disciples and friends. He is present to us in the sacraments and in the relationships of love that sustain our lives.

THE SEASON OF ADVENT

The season of Advent begins four Sundays before the Feast of Christmas. Its origin is a few centuries after the appearance of Christmas, generally thought to have originated in Spain, France, and northern Italy, and only later to have moved southward to the Church at Rome.

At the beginning of the fifth century we find a progressive development of theology leading up to Christmas in the many sermons of Saint Peter Chrysologus of Ravenna, in northern Italy. Just under a century later, under Pope Saint Gregory the Great—pope from 590–604—we find clear evidence of four Sunday Masses preceding the celebration of Christmas. The length of the season of Advent varied from place to place, but today it is generally three to four weeks long. It always begins four Sundays before December 25, and ends at the celebration of the birth of the Savior on that date.

THE COMING OF THE MESSIAH IN THE PAST

In the celebration of Advent we stand between two periods to which the readings of the season awaken us. The first significant period of time is in the *past*, and this is reflected primarily in the Gospel readings at Sunday Eucharist during the season. They look back to the anticipation of the coming of Jesus Christ into the world as one of us.

On the second Sunday of Advent, for example, all three Gospels (Year A from Matthew, Year B from Mark, Year C from Luke) proclaim the appearance of John the Baptist preparing the people for the coming of the Savior. The third Sunday's Gospels further the concentration on John the Baptist by having others approach John to ask him if he is indeed the Messiah, the one who is to come. John declares that he is not the Messiah but that the Messiah will soon be coming.

The fourth Sunday's Gospels have the annunciations to Joseph (in Matthew, Year A) and to Mary (in Luke, Years B and C) of the coming birth of Jesus. This Sunday's readings set us on the edge of our seats in anticipation of the birth narratives to be proclaimed on Christmas itself.

So, the past presence of God in the world is highlighted in the Gospels of Advent as we remember and celebrate the sequence of events in history leading up to the incarnation and birth of Jesus of Nazareth, a man like us in all things but sin.

THE COMING OF THE MESSIAH IN THE FUTURE

The other "period" of time highlighted in the season of Advent is the future: the Second Coming of Christ at the end of time. The time of this Second Coming is as unknown to us as the time of our own death; it may be tomorrow, or it may be a long time from now.

Early Christians expected that this return of the Messiah was going to happen soon, and this is one of the reasons why written evidence of the very earliest days of Christianity is so scant. Why bother to write these things down when the end of the world itself is around the corner? Only when these expectations were not realized did the next generations of Christians begin to write down what we now have as the New Testament collection of books.

Advent is unique in the liturgical year in its concentration on the end of the world. The readings of the liturgy that bring this concentration to the forefront are the second readings at the Eucharists celebrated in our parishes on the four Sundays of Advent. On the first Sunday of Advent in Year A, we hear a brief passage from Paul's Letter to the Romans:

> *You know the time in which we are living. It is now the hour for you to wake from sleep, for our salvation is closer than when we first accepted the faith. The night is far spent; the day draws near.*
>
> —Romans 13:11–12

As the season progresses the expectation of the end continues. In the Opening Prayer for the second Sunday of Advent we find:

> *Father in heaven,*
> *The day draws near when the glory of your Son will*
> *   make radiant the night of the waiting world.*

The Letter of James, proclaimed on the third Sunday of Advent in Year A, beseeches the community:

> *Be patient, my brothers, until the coming of the Lord. . . .*
> *Steady your hearts, because the coming of the Lord is*
> *   at hand.*
>
> —James 5:7, 8

Why are these two comings—the newborn Savior in the manger in Bethlehem and the glorious Second Coming at the end of the world—so closely linked in the Roman Catholic tradition?

Perhaps you have seen or heard preachers from non-Catholic churches—on street corners, in train stations, or on a Christian television or radio station—bidding the passersby to reform their ways because the Lord Jesus will be coming back, and soon, they assure us.

Such energetic and forbidding rhetoric can be frightening to Roman Catholics because we don't often hear such fiery preaching about the wrathful end of the world. Yet in our tradition the Second Coming of the Lord has never been absent. The consolation in finding it in the Advent season, however, is the juxtaposition of this return with the remembrance of the First Coming of the infant to Bethlehem.

THE CONSOLATION OF HIS COMING

At his First Coming, especially as this is narrated in the Gospel of Luke, the Savior and his mother Mary allied themselves with those who had little hope of the presence of God in their meager existences. Recall the song Mary proclaims after the angel Gabriel's announcement to her about the birth of her son, Jesus. In it Mary gives hope and light to those who have little:

> *My soul proclaims the greatness of the Lord;*
> *my spirit rejoices in God my Savior.*
> *For he has looked upon his handmaid's lowliness.*
>
> —Luke 1:46–48

She then continues by describing some of the reversals of fortune that have accompanied the coming of the Lord:

> *He has shown might with his arm,*
> *dispersed the arrogant of mind and heart.*
> *He has thrown down the rulers from their thrones*
> *but lifted up the lowly.*
> *The hungry he has filled with good things;*
> *the rich he has sent away empty.*
>
> —Luke 1:51–53

Our tradition has kept these reminders about the First Coming of the Lord so that we not get too carried away in fear by the anticipation of the Second Coming at the end of time. Our God was, is, and will be the same, then, now, and at the end of time. We will rejoice at the Lord's return.

FIERY JUDGE OF THE LIVING AND THE DEAD?

In spite of the consolation in the tradition at the juxtaposition of these two comings, Christian art through the centuries has tended to portray the Second Coming as that of a wrathful judge. In these depictions Jesus Christ sits in glory with the scrolls of the names of the dead on his knee. He sits there in judgment to separate the saved from the damned.

There are many reasons why such portraits have been part of our tradition; usually they arise from the threatening political and social circumstances of the author or painter. The tradition quietly reminds us of the long-held conviction of Catholic theology about the end of the world: It will not be a great surprise because we know its effect from what we have learned and experienced of the First Coming.

The season of Advent is a quiet annual reminder of what is to come. We can be consoled and peaceful rather than frightened and anxious.

THE SEASON OF CHRISTMAS

This period of time runs from the evening liturgy of Christmas Eve until the Sunday after the Feast of Epiphany, which is the Feast of the Baptism of the Lord. Within this season we find some very significant feast days.

Much of the significance of Christmas day itself was dealt with in the discussion of its possible origins. Yet we can also find much for reflection and prayer in its influence on human hearts and Christian life today. For many Christian communities today, as at Christmas' origins, December is one of the physically darkest and coldest times of the year. It is the natural time of the year when human beings would be reflecting on the sadnesses and complexities of life.

It is somewhat miraculous that in the midst of the tendency of the human mind to mirror the shadows of the Earth, we find a celebration of a modest birth in Bethlehem. It is the celebration of a vulnerable infant who was the Son of God, a cooing baby "wrapped in swaddling clothes," a youngster whose life was threatened by adversity yet whose life continues, 2,000 years later, to move people to courageous and heroic acts of virtue and strength.

Christmas at its heart is about new life emerging in the midst of terror, sadness, fear, and confusion. For this reason it is really a feast for us today.

It is true that the commercial frenzy that precedes and accompanies the feast moves us further and further away from the true meaning of the celebration. The greed that results in the acquisition of material goods is, by some oddness of the culture, directly opposed to the self-giving of the Savior that the feast prompts us to contemplate and imitate. But with those we love we can move ever closer to the values imbedded in the Matthean and Lukan stories of Jesus' birth. Doing so requires constant vigilance against the temptation to buy, buy, buy. We can be consoled by considering what in the end will last longer—the material possession for which we long, or the love that we share with family and loved ones.

The ancient image of Jesus as the Son of Justice can prompt us to activities during the Christmas season that will make Christmas special. Plan for you and your spouse (or boyfriend or girlfriend) and your children to do some concrete activity to realize justice—even to a small degree —in the world. Many volunteer agencies, which deliver food or healthcare to the sick in their homes, are shorthanded in the holiday season. Soup kitchens need help dishing out the meals. Or have your family or a group of friends sing carols on a street corner or pick up trash on the block. Odd? Certainly. But a gift to the world around you in a harsh season of the year? Absolutely. Such gifts will build strong opportunities and memories in your life.

THE DAYS AFTER CHRISTMAS

In the days immediately after Christmas Day itself, we celebrate commemorations of some of the most powerful saints within the Christian tradition. As we will see in the next chapter, these saints are all known to us from the stories about them in the New Testament, reflecting a priority in our tradition about saints who are in the Scriptures.

On December 26 we celebrate the Feast of Saint Stephen, the first martyr. What we know about Stephen is recorded in the Acts of the Apostles (chapters 6 and 7). The following day, on December 27, we celebrate the Feast of Saint John, follower of the Lord and, at least according to tradition, author of the Fourth Gospel. The very next day we celebrate the Feast of the Holy Innocents, a day on which we remember the anonymous children slain on the order of King Herod, who, seeking the life of the newborn Messiah, commanded that all children under two years old be killed in order to assure himself— to no avail—of the death of Jesus.

The Sunday after Christmas is the Feast of the Holy Family. It is a relatively recent addition to the calendar (nineteenth century) but is wholly fitting within the Christmas season. The secular year's beginning, January 1, is for Catholics the Feast of Mary, Mother of God.

THE FEAST OF THE EPIPHANY

We have already seen how the Feast of Epiphany was originally a celebration of the birth of Jesus. In the fourth century this was adopted by many churches, and since that time we have generally associated the coming of the Magi with the Feast of Epiphany.

The word *epiphaneia* means an "appearance" or "manifestation." In its origins the appearance to which the feast referred was not specified, and so the feast itself marked many appearances or manifestations—such as the birth of Jesus, the coming of the Magi, the baptism of Jesus, and the miracle at the wedding feast of Cana, and perhaps even the Transfiguration. While the others have not all lost their associations with the day, the remembrance of the Magi has come to be most prominent.

The Magi are significant not only because of their royal status as kings but because their travels from faraway lands cause us to consider the importance of spreading the message of Christ to distant people. The feast, therefore, has a missionary character to it.

The last major celebration of the Christmas season is the Feast of the Baptism of the Lord. There is virtually nothing recorded in the New Testament about the time between the infancy of Jesus and his adult life. As a recognition of this scriptural silence, the Church has the feast of his adult baptism in the Jordan River by John the Baptist closely connected to Christmas and following immediately after the Sunday marking the coming of the Magi.

The complexity of the study of the origins of Advent, Christmas, and Epiphany makes appreciating their significance tough. But the relative imprecision of dating techniques of the ancient world and the fluidity of the calendar of antiquity could make it nothing but complex.

Nevertheless, the Advent and Christmas seasons of the Church year are fascinating and, in their countercultural messages, prophetic about the presence of God in Christ and in the world. An appreciation of the complexity of the origins and developments of the feasts of Christmastime will provide some clue about the coming of God into our own lives: It may be complex and difficult to recognize, but it will bring much joy and light.

6 Saints in the Liturgical Year

As we turn to look at the place and the role of the saints in the liturgical year and in Christian spiritualities, we move into a new way of thinking about and keeping Catholic time. The other calendrical topics—Advent, Christmastime, the 40 days of Lent, the Triduum, and the 50 days of Eastertime—are not so much determined by dates as by "seasons" or "periods," periods that often begin and/or end on the Lord's Day, Sunday.

Four Sundays before the celebration of Christmas we mark the first Sunday of Advent no matter what the calendar date of that Sunday may be. The same is true of the Feast of the Baptism of the Lord, which ends the Christmas season on a Sunday. They are always during the same *season* of the year, but they are more dependent on the time of the year and the day of the week than they are on the calendar's date. The same is true of the Sundays of Lent, of the Three Days at the center of the liturgical year (which always embrace the period from Thursday through Sunday evening), and of the Sundays of the Easter season. This "seasonal" schedule is called the *temporal cycle* in Church teaching, coming from the Latin word *tempora*, meaning "season" or "period."

The seasons of the Church year that we have already looked at comprise the temporal cycle of liturgical observances. There is an aspect to the Catholic calendar, however, that overlaps and even conflicts with the temporal cycle, and this is the *sanctoral cycle*, coming from the Latin words *sanctus* and *sancta*, meaning "saint." As we move into a consideration of the calendar of the saints, we adhere very closely to dates rather than seasons.

The Feast of Saint Joseph, the husband of Mary and father of Jesus, for example, is always on March 19. Well, almost always. There is one exception to the dates of the sanctoral cycle: During years when they happen on Sundays, the feast day of a particular saint is usually displaced by the Sunday celebration, especially during the special seasons of the year. But for the most part, the dates of the feasts of the saints are constants once they are set in the calendar.

CHANGES IN THE SANCTORAL CYCLE

Unlike the seasons of the liturgical years, for which we do not notice much change as time goes by, the sanctoral cycle does in fact admit of noticeable change. In this regard, however, the changes are not today as they were in the recent past.

THE INFLUENCE OF JOHN PAUL II

The papacy of John Paul II brought about more changes than ever before in the calendar of the saints and even in the process of canonization of holy people. For one thing, during his papacy more persons were canonized than under any other pope in Christian history. One of the differences between canonizations now and those a few decades ago is that few, if any, canonizations these days become part of the *universal* Catholic calendar.

UNIVERSAL SAINTS

There are some saints, of course, whose lives so influenced the Church worldwide—Mary Magdalene, Matthew, Mark, Luke, John, Francis of Assisi and his follower Clare, and so on—that they are part of the universal calendar.

Such saints are universal in celebration either because they are saints whose stories are told in sacred Scripture, or they are saints whose holiness was so well known that this saint, like Saint Francis, is celebrated all around the world.

But now the Church recognizes the canonizations of persons even if devotion to them and to their holy example will not be celebrated everywhere. Today, many canonizations are marked only in the countries or regions or continents on which the saints themselves lived.

Another remarkable change in the sanctoral cycle under the papacy of John Paul II is the broadening of the horizons around who is going to be canonized. Though the Church still has a long way to go, much has changed. Before his papacy most of those who were canonized were bishops, nuns, priests, leaders of religious communities, and celibates. It is not that these Church leaders were not holy, but they weren't the only ones in Christian history to be holy! The Church now advocates causes of lay persons more strongly than ever before.

PLACE OF ORIGIN

In addition to changing the demographics regarding the type of vocation in the Church suitable for persons who might be canonized, the places from which the persons themselves come has shifted. Until 20 or 30 years ago, nearly every single person who was canonized was of European origin. Many, especially those who were missionaries, did not live their whole lives in Europe but almost 100 percent hailed from Europe by birth. John Paul has helped shift this. Under his tenure as pope, many persons were canonized from other parts of the world, such as Asia, Africa, and South America.

Furthermore, the lifestyle of persons being canonized in the past was almost identical: a celibate member of a religious community or a celibate priest. And far too many of the canonized have been men. This, too, has begun to change. More women are being considered for the process of canonization; also, the causes of more married persons are being considered. For the first time ever in Christianity, for example, a married couple is under investigation for the process of canonization.

CAN MARRIED PEOPLE BE HOLY PEOPLE?

The cause of Louis and Azélie Martin—the parents of Saint Thérèse of Lisieux, the "Little Flower," who died in 1897 at the age of 24—for canonization is in process. Thérèse herself wrote an autobiography, *The Life of a Soul*, chronicling her time in the convent and her trust in God when she accepted the fate of her early and painful death from tuberculosis.

Her parents were such strong influences on her life and on her vocation that they are now up for canonization. The Martins is just one of the many extraordinarily surprising cases that are being studied by the Congregation for the Causes of Saints.

THE BIRTH OF THE OFFICIAL PROCESS OF CANONIZATION

The relatively bureaucratic procedure for canonizations is not as ancient as most people think. It arose from adverse circumstances at the time of the Reformation. When Protestant communities were breaking away from their former Catholic ties, there were many issues they sought to reform, and many of these had to do with worship.

One of the most problematic issues with Catholic worship was the calendar because it was filled with many saints. This had happened because there was little in the way of official approval of those whose lives were remembered and celebrated in the calendar. Popular acclaim was the main way in which holy persons—and some not-so-holy persons—became saints in the Church.

When the theologians of the Reformation started to envision their theology, they drew their notion from the First Letter to Timothy, which states:

There is one God.
There is also one mediator between God and the
human race,
Christ Jesus, himself human,
who gave himself as ransom for all.

—1 Timothy 2:5–6

It is indeed true that through Jesus Christ alone came our salvation. The reformers of the sixteenth century found this to be in contradiction to the veneration given to the saints in the Catholic Church. Either there was *one* mediator, Jesus Christ, or there were many, the saints.

Reacting to the challenges from the reformers, the Catholic Church began to develop the process by which a person would legitimately become a saint in the tradition. The process, they hoped, would eliminate some of the stranger saints in the tradition, those whose holiness might indeed be hard to come upon. The Church also was trying to pare down the calendar so that the temporal cycle was not so often displaced by the commemoration of the saints.

The Congregation for the Causes of Saints was introduced into the Church in 1588, only 400 years ago. That's only one-quarter of Christian history. For the first 1,500 years of the tradition, the sanctoral cycle was a local thing, usually involving the bishop and perhaps some priests and lay investigators, but not with the seriousness and rigor of the process since 1588.

WHO'S WHO IN THE CALENDAR OF THE SAINTS?

In the calendar of the entire Church we find either saints who are in the Bible—Mary and Joseph, the disciples, Mary Magdalene, Martha and Mary, etc.—or those who wrote books of the New Testament—Paul, Timothy, and so on.

There, too, we also find particular celebrations of Mary, the mother of Jesus: We find the Feast of Mary, the Mother of God (January 1); feasts like the Immaculate Conception (December 8), the Annunciation (March 25), and the Assumption of Mary into Heaven (August 15).

THE SAINTS AND DAILY CELEBRATIONS OF THE EUCHARIST IN THE PARISH

Although not many days in the sanctoral cycle displace the Sunday eucharistic celebrations, the saints are often remembered and their lives and examples celebrated in the weekday liturgies, Monday to Saturday. In addition to the Scriptures and Catholic theology, the lives of the saints can provide fascinating material for preaching at daily Mass. The depths to which the observance is marked can vary, according to the relationship of the parish community to that particular saint. Let's consider an example and some of the circumstances of parishes that might celebrate a feast in different ways.

February 10 is the Feast of Saint Scholastica. Scholastica was the twin sister of Saint Benedict, who is popularly known as the founder of Western monasticism. Scholastica founded a women's community of monks not far from the community her brother founded at Monte Cassino in Italy. As the pastoral team in a certain parish—liturgy director, priest, lector, eucharistic minister, cantor, etc.—is considering the liturgical options for the coming week, they come to plan February 10, which is on a weekday.

If they elect to observe the Feast of Saint Scholastica, they can start the observation by using the right color of vestment (white) and, perhaps, altar cloths. At the same time, the presider should pray the opening and closing prayers for that feast. These are the minimum requirements for memorializing Scholastica on February 10.

If the community wants to take the observance still another step further, it might write an intercession about monks, nuns, virgins, or about monastic vocations in the Church to mark the occasion. The community also can suspend the proclamation of readings that would usually be read at the weekday liturgy and choose readings from the Common of Virgins. These readings would reflect even more the feast being celebrated, but this should be done only if for a specific purpose, because doing so has the faith community abandoning the *lectio continua*, the continual reading through the Gospels that happens in the course of the weekday Masses.

In addition to the modifications that can be chosen for the liturgy of the word, the eucharistic prayer can also be chosen and modified with Scholastica's name to reflect her memorial in the prayer of the Church still further. By so making these plans in anticipation of the feast, the day can be a tremendous opportunity to catechize about a particular period of Church history (the sixth century, during which both Scholastica and her brother lived in Italy) and about a particular aspect of our rich Christian tradition, monasticism, which is still alive and strong, over a millennium and a half after its beginnings in Egypt in the fourth and fifth centuries. This variety in the sanctoral cycle of people from many different walks of life and from many different places is a wonderful chance for enriching the faith lives of those who celebrate daily Eucharist in the parish.

At the same time, we can keep in mind that too much celebration can weaken its importance. If everyday is a special day, the special days themselves will start to be quite ordinary.

A further aspect of the example of February 10 would be taken into account if, for example, your parish was in fact the Church of Saint Scholastica. February 10 would then be the matronal feast of your community, and a significant observance (which might include more singing and solemnity) would be appropriate.

It's possible, too, that your church might not be named Scholastica or Benedict but that it is staffed by Benedictine men and women (those who've committed themselves for life to a community that lives by the Rule of Saint Benedict). For these men and women, February 10 is a very significant day, and the parishioners of their parish should share in the celebration with them, particularly in the celebration of a strong, vibrant liturgy, eucharistic or not.

There might be other ways in which the veneration of this saint would be observed, if, for example, there is a Catholic women's support group called The Women of Saint Scholastica (or something akin to this), or if the local Catholic girls' high school was called Saint Scholastica. The specificity of the life of Scholastica would be traditionally engaging, and it can be drawn on to connect the parish to the saint by which it was named, and thereby to connect the members of the parish to each other.

Scholastica is just one of the many saints in the history of the Church at whose life we might have looked. But, as stated above, it's important to be selective in observing liturgically the life of a saint. That a saint's memorial exists doesn't mean that it has to be observed, and it needn't be observed each year with the same solemnity or sparity, if observed at all.

WHAT THE SAINTS BRING TO OUR FAITH

As we've seen, under the reform of the canonization process in the papacy of John Paul II, saints are no longer made saints for Catholic churches everywhere. At the time of the Reformation and continuing up until the time of Vatican II, the sanctoral calendar was heavy. Rarely, if ever, did a liturgical day pass without an interrupting celebration of a saint's feast or memorial, and these were ranked in a rather complex system of observance.

After the reform of the liturgy following Vatican II, the Church eliminated the sanctorally heavy calendar in order for those attending daily Mass to get a better idea of the progression of the seasons and times of the liturgical year, independent of the sanctoral cycle. The reform of the Lectionary after Vatican II brought the sacred Scriptures into the vernacular languages and added far more Scripture readings, especially for those who celebrated the Eucharist daily in their parish. With the wealth added to the liturgy by the new Lectionary and its lengthy cycles—a three-year cycle (A, B, C) for Sundays and a two-year cycle (I, II) for weekdays—the sanctoral cycle was pared down.

Saints of particular places are now celebrated with vigor and enthusiasm in the places where that person was and is well known, but a memorial for the saint is not observed in places where neither the presider nor the other celebrants know who that saint is. When the celebrations are planned with care and foresight, the sanctoral cycle and the life of the saints accessible through it bring diversity to our understanding of holiness, of the relationship between culture and faith, and even of our appreciation of a holy life actualized day after day according to the liturgical, scriptural, and theological traditions of the Church. In other words, the saints reveal for us in a new way the presence of God in the world.

ONE MEDIATOR, MANY SAINTS

Jesus Christ was and is our one mediator. Yet Jesus lived in a concrete time and place, a place with cultural and historical particularities and idiosyncracies that are not always as accessible to all people who come to know of him.

One of the benefits that the saints can provide for us is making the Gospel have a concretization in a time and place that may be more accessible to someone coming to Christian faith for the first time or for someone returning after a time away from the faith. The stories of heroic and admirable characters and their witness to the faith in adverse circumstances are engaging for Catholic children, indeed for all Catholic believers.

The tradition of venerating the saints goes back to the age of martyrdom in the first few centuries of Christian history. It is most fruitful in parish life when it is attended to with planning and strong preaching. The witness of the lives of the saints has brought many people to the faith from its earliest days. And even after the many changes in the process of canonization in the past few decades, the saints still bring vitality to Christian life.

Conclusion

L ike liturgy itself, the liturgical year is not for God but for us believers. It enables us to be mindful of and thankful for God's presence in our lives. It provides us with strength and consolation in the ups and downs of human life.

The purpose of the structure and nuances of the liturgical year is not to prompt us to figure out *exactly* when it is that God will be most available to help us in times of need. This is not necessary because, as sacred Scripture assures us in many places, God is always there for us.

The purpose of the liturgical year—a rather complex rendering of time by any standard—is to remind us that God is present for us. Throughout Christianity there have been and are times when the past or the present or the future of God's presence are emphasized at the expense of the other two. It is easier to remember God's presence in the past, especially in the life of Jesus of Nazareth. And it is comparably easier to anticipate the future time of God's presence, when the Messiah will return again.

The hardest aspect for us of the relationship of faith and time is finding the presence of God in the present, in our own sometimes ordinary 24-hour days. But our faith tells us that, after the coming of the Lord Jesus, we have access to the life of God as it comes to us in the Church and in the humanity we share with all other persons. The narratives and celebrations of the liturgical year that we've considered will prompt us to find the presence of God incarnate in our own lives through Jesus Christ and in the Church.

The feasts that we've considered have narratives assigned to them for our uplifting and inspiration. The traditions of the liturgical year go back centuries, some going back—in different forms—even before the life of Jesus on Earth. Sometimes the content and gestures of the liturgy carry on a very long heritage that believers have left with us. Maintaining them by giving glory to God, from whom all good blessings flow, is the purpose of the Church's liturgical year. The liturgical year is both unwavering and ever new. And it makes our lives of faith the same.